A
Book Lover's
Journal

A
Book Lover's
Journal

Addison-Wesley Publishing Company, Inc.

Reading, Massachusetts   Menlo Park, California   New York

Don Mills, Ontario   Wokingham, England   Amsterdam

Bonn   Sydney   Singapore   Tokyo   Madrid   San Juan

Many giving people lent their hands to this project, and the editors here wish to thank them all and to acknowledge especially the help of Jill Erickson, Harry Katz, and Sally M. Pierce of the Boston Athenæum; John Y. Coles and Peter Van Wingan of the Library of Congress; Susan Halpert of the Houghton Library, Harvard University; Dr. M. A. Halls of King's College Library; Alfred Lane of the William H. and Gwynne K. Crouse Library for Publishing Arts, City University of New York; Kenneth Gloss of the Brattle Book Shop; and Leo Marks.

Thanks also to the following publishers: to Harcourt Brace Jovanovich, for permission to quote from "In My Library" in *Two Cheers for Democracy* by E. M. Forster, copyright © 1951 by E. M. Forster, renewed 1979 by Donald Perry; to Harvard University Press, for permission to reprint from *One Writer's Beginnings* by Eudora Welty, copyright © 1983, 1984 by Eudora Welty; and to Random House, Inc., for permission to quote from *At Random: The Reminiscences of Bennett Cerf* by Bennett Cerf, copyright © 1977 by Random House, Inc., and from the foreword to *The Faulkner Reader* by William Faulkner, copyright © 1954 by William Faulkner.

The engraving on the back cover is by Jost Amman (1588), and the frontispiece is from a lithograph by Paul Gavarni (1858). Both images are reproduced courtesy of the Boston Athenæum.

ISBN 0–201–10354–0

FGHIJ-DO-93210

Sixth printing, May 1990

"Sitting last winter among my books, and walled round with all the comfort and protection which they and my fireside could afford me,—to wit, a table of high-piled books at my back, my writing desk on one side of me, some shelves on the other, and the feeling of the warm fire at my feet, —I began to consider how I loved the authors of those books; how I loved them too, not only for the imaginative pleasures they afforded me, but for their making me love the very books themselves, and delight to be in contact with them. I looked sideways at my Spenser, my Theocritus, and my *Arabian Nights*; then above them at my Italian Poets; and behind me at my Dryden and Pope, my Romances, and my Boccaccio; then on my left side at my Chaucer, who lay on my writing desk; and thought how natural it was in Charles Lamb to give a kiss to an old folio, as I once saw him do to Chapman's Homer."

Leigh Hunt, from his essay "My Books"

Before a book is a novel or journal or anything else, it is by definition a gathering of sheets, usually of paper. Since paper was first invented in the Orient about two thousand years ago, the basic steps in making it have remained much the same, and the centuries-old method depicted in this woodcut is still used by fine papermakers. A raw material—wood, rags—is pulped and suspended in a vat of water. A fine mesh in a frame—the paper mold—is plunged into the vat and when pulled out holds a sheet of matted fibers. Each new sheet is laid on a piece of felt and the felts stacked high for the press. When, after many pressings, the excess water has been squeezed out, the paper is hung to dry.

Woodcut from Seikichirō Gotō's Journey of Paper *(Japan, 1964)*

TITLE _____

AUTHOR _____

DATE READ _____

COMMENTS _____

_____

_____

_____

_____

_____

_____

_____

_____

_____

_____

_____

_____

_____

_____

_____

_____

_____

_____

_____

_____

_____

_____

_____

_____

_____

TITLE _____

AUTHOR _____

DATE READ _____

COMMENTS _____

_____

_____

_____

_____

_____

_____

_____

_____

_____

_____

_____

_____

_____

_____

_____

_____

_____

_____

_____

_____

_____

_____

_____

_____

_____

_____

The first printed book, a Latin Bible of over twelve hundred pages, was completed in Mainz, Germany, in 1455. The grand architect of the Bible, Johannes Gutenberg (c. 1397–1468), was also the inventor of the tools with which it was printed—a wooden press, oil-based printing ink, and, most originally, movable metal type cast from molds. Gutenberg's Bible is, however, something more than the first fruit of a tremendous technological innovation—it is among the greatest masterpieces of the printer's art. Its black and masculine type, designed and cut by Gutenberg, is based on letter forms of the finest scribes of medieval Germany, and the craft that went into the book's composition, illuminated initials, and pressmanship is equal to that of any later master. The Bible was printed on vellum in an edition of perhaps two hundred copies, forty-seven of which have survived the centuries.

Gutenberg Taking the First Proof, *an engraving published in 1869 by John Fry & Company, New York, courtesy of the Library of Congress*

TITLE _____

AUTHOR _____

DATE READ _____

COMMENTS _____

_____

_____

_____

_____

_____

_____

_____

_____

_____

_____

_____

_____

_____

_____

_____

_____

_____

_____

_____

_____

_____

_____

_____

_____

_____

_____

_____

_____

_____

TITLE _____

AUTHOR _____

DATE READ _____

COMMENTS _____

_____

_____

_____

_____

_____

_____

_____

_____

_____

_____

_____

_____

_____

_____

_____

_____

_____

_____

_____

_____

_____

_____

_____

_____

_____

TITLE _____

AUTHOR _____

DATE READ _____

COMMENTS _____

_____

_____

_____

_____

_____

_____

_____

_____

_____

_____

_____

_____

_____

_____

William Caxton (c. 1422–1491) was a British trade diplomat, but after-hours he devoted to literature, especially to making English versions of his favorite French romances. While on business in Cologne in the early 1470s he learned how to print and by 1474 had set up his own press in Bruges. The following year he produced the first printed book in English, his translation of Raoul le Fèure's *Recueil des histoires de Troye*; he is pictured here presenting a copy to Margaret, duchess of Burgundy. In 1476 he returned to England and established a press, the first on the island, in Westminster. There he printed some one hundred titles, among them *The Canterbury Tales* and his translation of Malory's *Morte d'Arthur*. By making large numbers of books in English available for the first time, he exerted a shaping influence on the language.

TITLE _____

AUTHOR _____

DATE READ _____

COMMENTS _____

_____

_____

_____

_____

_____

_____

_____

_____

_____

_____

_____

_____

"He's having all his books translated into French. They lose
something in the original."

TITLE _____

AUTHOR _____

DATE READ _____

COMMENTS _____

_____

_____

_____

_____

_____

_____

_____

_____

_____

_____

_____

_____

_____

_____

_____

_____

_____

_____

_____

_____

_____

_____

_____

_____

TITLE _____

AUTHOR _____

DATE READ _____

COMMENTS _____

_____

_____

_____

_____

_____

_____

_____

_____

_____

_____

_____

_____

_____

_____

_____

_____

_____

_____

_____

_____

_____

_____

_____

_____

_____

_____

TITLE _____

AUTHOR _____

DATE READ _____

COMMENTS _____

_____

_____

_____

_____

_____

_____

_____

_____

_____

_____

_____

_____

_____

_____

_____

_____

_____

_____

_____

_____

_____

_____

_____

_____

_____

_____

_____

TITLE _____

AUTHOR _____

DATE READ _____

COMMENTS _____

_____

_____

_____

_____

_____

_____

_____

Hamilton and Company was one of eighteenth-century England's most successful booksellers. It incorporated the Shakespeare Library, which offered members both a reading room and a large collection of books for rent, indispensable services at a time when the country had no free public libraries.   *Anonymous woodcut, circa 1790, courtesy of the Boston Athenæum*

TITLE _____

AUTHOR _____

DATE READ _____

COMMENTS _____

_____

_____

_____

_____

_____

_____

_____

_____

_____

_____

_____

_____

_____

_____

_____

_____

_____

_____

_____

_____

_____

_____

_____

_____

_____

_____

_____

_____

_____

_____

As children, the Brontës—Charlotte, Branwell, Emily, and Anne—authored a family library of tiny books chronicling the fantasy kingdoms of Angria and Gondal. Charlotte (1816–1855), who later wrote *Jane Eyre* and *Villette,* made the volumes pictured here: they were penned in a minute script resembling bookprint and were hand sewn into covers made from sugar bags and scraps of wallpaper.

Photograph by Simon Warner, copyright © The Brontë Society

TITLE _____

AUTHOR _____

DATE READ _____

COMMENTS _____

_____

_____

_____

_____

_____

_____

_____

_____

_____

_____

_____

_____

_____

_____

_____

_____

_____

_____

_____

_____

_____

_____

_____

_____

_____

_____

_____

TITLE _____

AUTHOR _____

DATE READ _____

COMMENTS _____

_____

_____

_____

_____

_____

_____

_____

_____

_____

_____

_____

_____

_____

_____

_____

_____

_____

_____

_____

_____

_____

_____

_____

_____

_____

TITLE _____

AUTHOR _____

DATE READ _____

COMMENTS _____

_____

_____

_____

_____

_____

_____

_____

_____

_____

_____

_____

_____

_____

_____

_____

_____

_____

_____

_____

_____

_____

_____

_____

_____

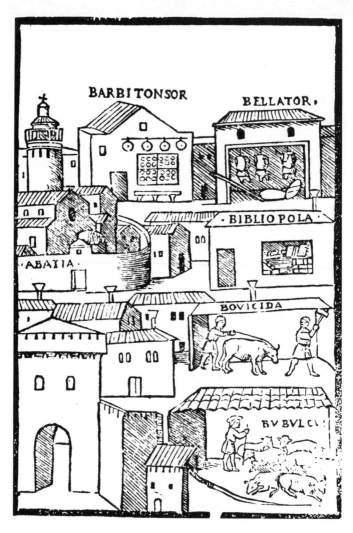

This Venetian woodblock print, circa 1533, contains the earliest known picture of a bookseller's storefront. Labeled *bibliopola* (or, if you will, "book city") the shop looks strikingly modern—right down to its window display— among the shops of such other tradesmen as an armor maker and a cow slayer.

Woodcut attributed to Johannes Romberch, courtesy of the Boston Athenæum

TITLE _____

AUTHOR _____

DATE READ _____

COMMENTS _____

_____

_____

_____

_____

_____

_____

_____

_____

_____

_____

_____

_____

_____

_____

_____

_____

_____

_____

_____

_____

_____

_____

_____

_____

_____

_____

_____

_____

_____

_____

TITLE _____

AUTHOR _____

DATE READ _____

COMMENTS _____

_____

_____

_____

_____

_____

_____

_____

_____

AL   DVS

Both the rise of the humanistic tradition in the West and the very look of the modern book owe an inestimable debt to the work of one man, Aldus Manutius of Venice (1450–1515). He and his sons after him printed hundreds of volumes of the Greek and Latin classics and, alone among Renaissance printers, assembled a staff of editors, the Aldine Academy, to insure their books' textual accuracy. They published, in most cases for the first time, the works of Aeschylus, Sophocles, Euripides, Thucydides,

TITLE _____

AUTHOR _____

DATE READ _____

COMMENTS _____

_____

_____

_____

_____

_____

_____

_____

_____

_____

and Plato; Aristotle, Horace, and Pliny; Plutarch, Dante, and Erasmus—in short, a complete scholarly library of the greatest ancient and contemporary literature.

Aldus's books were as significant for their typography as for their content. At a time when most books were unwieldy volumes meant to be read at lecterns, Aldus specialized in portable books, printed in large numbers and sold at affordable prices. Their pages were simple and clean in design, and the types—including the first italics, cut for Aldus by Francesco Griffo (1450–1518)—remarkable for their versatility and legibility. Well distributed throughout all of Europe, extraordinarily successful with readers and booksellers, Aldine editions were the "paperbacks" of their day.

TITLE _____

AUTHOR _____

DATE READ _____

COMMENTS _____

_____

_____

_____

_____

_____

_____

_____

_____

_____

_____

_____

_____

_____

_____

_____

_____

_____

_____

_____

_____

_____

_____

_____

_____

_____

_____

TITLE _____

AUTHOR _____

DATE READ _____

COMMENTS _____

_____

_____

_____

_____

_____

_____

_____

_____

_____

_____

_____

_____

_____

_____

_____

_____

_____

_____

_____

_____

_____

_____

_____

_____

_____

_____

TITLE _____

AUTHOR _____

DATE READ _____

COMMENTS _____

In 1800, the English draftsman Thomas Rowlandson attended a book sale at Sotheby's and made this immortal study of certain of his countrymen suffering the advanced stages of bibliomania. Sotheby's, now the world's leading firm of art auctioneers and appraisers, opened for business in 1744 as a book auction house.   *Drawing copyright © by Sotheby's, Inc.*

TITLE _____

AUTHOR _____

DATE READ _____

COMMENTS _____

_____

_____

_____

_____

_____

_____

_____

_____

THE
VVHOLE
BOOKE OF PSALMES
Faithfully
TRANSLATED *into* ENGLISH
Metre.

Whereunto is prefixed a difcourfe declaring not only the lawfullnes, but alfo
the neceffity of the heavenly Ordinance
of finging Scripture Pfalmes in
the Churches of
God.

Coll. III.

*Let the word of God dwell plenteoufly in
you, in all wifdome, teaching and exhort-
ing one another in Pfalmes, Himnes, and
fpirituall Songs, finging to the Lord with
grace in your hearts.*

Iames V.

*If any be afflicted, let him pray, and if
any be merry let bim fing pfalmes.*

Imprinted
1640

TITLE _____

AUTHOR _____

DATE READ _____

COMMENTS _____

_____

_____

_____

_____

_____

_____

_____

_____

_____

_____

_____

_____

_____

_____

_____

_____

_____

In 1638, the Reverend José Glover sailed from England for Massachusetts to establish himself as the first printer in the colonies. He died on the journey, but his plan for a press was carried out by his widow, who inherited his machinery, and by Stephen Daye, a locksmith he'd employed to man it. Daye and his son Matthew set up an office in the house of Henry Dunster, the first president of Harvard College in Cambridge, and by January 1639 had printed a broadside, "The Freeman's Oath." It was followed the next year by *The Whole Booke of Psalmes*—known as *The Bay Psalm Book*—the first book in English printed in North America. A pocket-size volume of 296 pages, it was issued in an edition of 1,700 copies of which only eleven are known to have survived.

TITLE _____

AUTHOR _____

DATE READ _____

COMMENTS _____

_____

_____

_____

_____

_____

_____

_____

_____

_____

_____

_____

_____

_____

_____

_____

_____

_____

_____

_____

_____

_____

_____

_____

_____

_____

_____

TITLE _____

AUTHOR _____

DATE READ _____

COMMENTS _____

_____

_____

_____

_____

_____

_____

_____

_____

_____

_____

_____

_____

_____

_____

_____

_____

_____

_____

_____

_____

_____

_____

_____

_____

TITLE _____

AUTHOR _____

DATE READ _____

COMMENTS _____

_____

_____

_____

_____

_____

_____

_____

_____

_____

_____

_____

_____

John Baskerville of Birmingham (1706–1775) made his fortune crafting japanned enamelware, but in his mid-forties he retired to pursue an obsession: "Having been an early admirer of the beauty of Letters, I became insensibly desirous of contributing to the perfection of them." He spent seven years designing the alphabet that bears his name, a beautifully balanced and extraordinarily legible typeface still widely used today. Pictured are a Baskerville specimen page and some original punches now in the collection of Cambridge University.

Photograph courtesy of Cambridge University Library, used with permission of Cambridge University Press

Two-line Do
ndem aliquando,
andem aliq
Great Prim
A B C
ndem aliquando, Quiri

TITLE _____

AUTHOR _____

DATE READ _____

COMMENTS _____

_____

_____

_____

_____

_____

_____

_____

_____

_____

_____

_____

_____

At age twenty-eight, Giambattista Bodoni (1740–1813), a talented punch cutter for a Catholic missionary press, was invited by the duke of Parma to direct the Stamperia Reale, the official printer to the court. Freed from all financial considerations and given full artistic freedom, Bodoni conceived grand projects and his genius for book and letter design quickly flourished. For the Stamperia, he designed over three hundred typefaces, including the roman one which bears his name; most all of them are included in his magnificent folio *Manuale tipografico* (1788). Never has a typographer been more celebrated in his time: he was invited to the Vatican by the Pope, his works collected by the world's aristocracy, and he was given pensions by Napoleon and the king of Spain. The city of Parma built a museum to house his life's work and struck a medal in his honor.

Engraving of a monument to Bodoni erected at Saluzzo in 1872, courtesy of the Library of Congress

TITLE _____

AUTHOR _____

DATE READ _____

COMMENTS _____

_____

_____

_____

_____

_____

_____

_____

_____

_____

_____

_____

_____

_____

_____

_____

_____

_____

_____

_____

_____

_____

_____

_____

_____

_____

_____

_____

TITLE _____

AUTHOR _____

DATE READ _____

COMMENTS _____

_____

_____

_____

_____

_____

_____

_____

_____

_____

_____

_____

_____

_____

_____

_____

_____

_____

_____

_____

_____

_____

_____

_____

_____

TITLE _____

AUTHOR _____

DATE READ _____

COMMENTS _____

_____

_____

_____

_____

_____

_____

_____

_____

_____

_____

_____

_____

_____

_____

_____

Benjamin Franklin (1706–1790) is perhaps best remembered as a scientist and diplomat, but he thought of himself as above all else a printer, the proprietor of the most successful press in Philadelphia. He published and edited the widely-read *Pennsylvania Gazette* and was the printer of the colony's currency, but his favorite items from his press were books, some of which he designed himself. Much of his work was done on a press like the one pictured here, the press on which he was apprenticed in London and which is now in the Smithsonian Institution.   *Photograph courtesy of the Library of Congress*

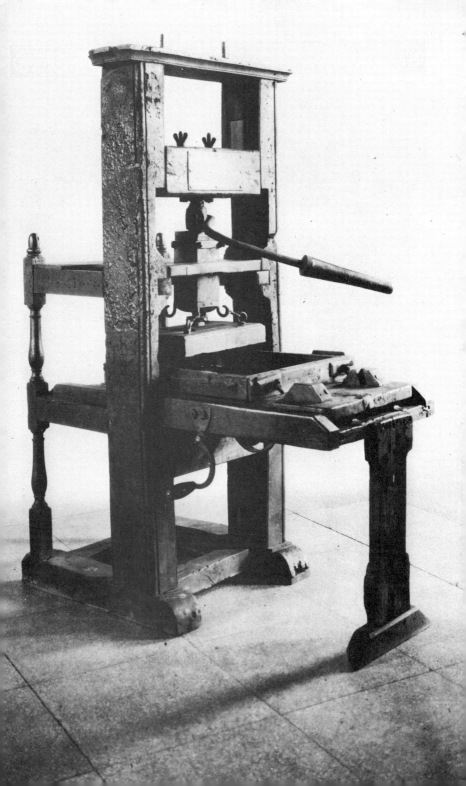

During the mid-nineteenth century, America called it Parnassus Corner, the corner of Boston that held the bookstore of William D. Ticknor and James T. Fields. On its ground floor, Hawthorne, Emerson, Longfellow, and Thoreau purchased each other's books; upstairs, Ticknor and Fields published them. Ticknor was a pillar of business integrity and good sense and Fields, in the words of Henry James, was "addicted to the cultivation of talk and wit and to the ingenious multiplication of such ties as could link the top half of the title-page with the lower." They were the greatest American publishers of their time, and the Old Corner perhaps the greatest bookstore.

Anonymous etching, circa 1835, courtesy of the Boston Athenæum

TITLE _____

AUTHOR _____

DATE READ _____

COMMENTS _____

_____

_____

_____

_____

_____

_____

_____

_____

_____

_____

_____

_____

_____

_____

_____

_____

_____

_____

_____

_____

_____

_____

_____

_____

_____

_____

TITLE _____

AUTHOR _____

DATE READ _____

COMMENTS _____

_____

_____

_____

_____

_____

_____

_____

_____

_____

_____

_____

_____

_____

_____

_____

_____

_____

_____

_____

_____

_____

_____

_____

_____

_____

_____

TITLE _____

AUTHOR _____

DATE READ _____

COMMENTS _____

_____

_____

_____

_____

_____

_____

_____

_____

_____

_____

_____

_____

_____

_____

_____

_____

_____

_____

_____

_____

_____

_____

_____

_____

Upon retirement from service as the King's Secretary for Admiralty Affairs, Samuel Pepys devoted himself to amassing a personal library of three thousand items, much of it collected as reference material for his projected history of the English navy. He never got far with the writing, but the fourteen years before his death in 1703 were a long, blissful book hunter's holiday for him. Agents and relatives joined him in a pan-European search for rare materials which he and a hired librarian catalogued in Pepys's house in Westminster; Pepys commissioned new title pages and indexes for most of the books and ran down appropriate prints and drawings to illustrate them. He left the library to his alma mater, Magdalene College, under the restriction that it be forever housed in the twelve glazed-front oak bookcases he had had specially built for it, and forever arranged in the system he and his associate devised. On the back row of the second shelf of the first of these bookcases sit the six quarto volumes of the diary Pepys kept between his twenty-seventh and thirty-sixth years. His biographer, Arthur Bryant, called the diary "far more than an ordinary record of its writer's thoughts and actions; it is a supreme work of art . . . and it is probably, after the Bible and James Boswell's *Life of Samuel Johnson*, the best bedside book in the English language." Above are its opening pages, written in the Shelton system of shorthand and dated January 1, 1660.

TITLE _____

AUTHOR _____

DATE READ _____

COMMENTS _____

_____

_____

_____

_____

_____

_____

_____

_____

_____

_____

_____

_____

_____

_____

_____

_____

_____

_____

_____

_____

_____

_____

_____

_____

_____

_____

_____

_____

TITLE _____

AUTHOR _____

DATE READ _____

COMMENTS _____

_____

_____

_____

_____

_____

_____

_____

_____

_____

_____

_____

_____

_____

_____

_____

_____

_____

_____

_____

_____

_____

_____

_____

_____

_____

_____

The Boston Athenæum, perhaps America's most famous subscription library, was founded in 1807 by the editors of *The Monthly Anthology and Boston Review*. Its present home at 10½ Beacon Street was built in 1847 and originally consisted of three floors, only the second of which held books; the other floors held the paintings and statuary on which the collection of the Boston Museum of Fine Arts was built. Now five densely-packed floors high, the Athenæum houses some 700,000 volumes, including most of the personal libraries of George Washington and John Quincy Adams.

Photograph by Jackson Smith of the Athenæum's Members' Reading Room, courtesy of the Boston Athenæum

TITLE _____

AUTHOR _____

DATE READ _____

COMMENTS _____

TITLE _____

AUTHOR _____

DATE READ _____

COMMENTS _____

_____

_____

_____

_____

_____

_____

_____

_____

_____

_____

_____

_____

_____

_____

_____

_____

_____

_____

_____

_____

_____

_____

_____

_____

_____

_____

_____

_____

The Linotype machine, invented in Baltimore in the 1880s by German immigrant Ottmar Mergenthaler, was perfected and mass-produced by the late 1920s. It radically increased the speed with which a line of type could be composed. Its operator punches keys much like a typewriter's, letter matrices rattle into place in a composing chamber, the matrices receive a pressurized stream of molten lead, and an entire line of type is cast in a single slug—all within seconds. The machine put an abrupt end to almost four centuries of setting type by hand but is a lumbering dinosaur beside today's electronic phototypesetters.

Photograph courtesy of the Library of Congress

TITLE _____

AUTHOR _____

DATE READ _____

COMMENTS _____

_____

_____

_____

_____

_____

_____

_____

_____

_____

_____

_____

_____

_____

_____

_____

_____

_____

_____

_____

_____

_____

_____

_____

_____

_____

_____

_____

_____

_____

TITLE _____

AUTHOR _____

DATE READ _____

COMMENTS _____

_____

_____

_____

_____

_____

_____

_____

_____

_____

_____

_____

_____

_____

_____

_____

_____

_____

_____

_____

_____

_____

_____

_____

_____

Sam Clemens (1835–1910), alias Mark Twain, made a fortune writing
books, then lost it publishing them. His fascination with the mechanics
of bookmaking began with a job as a printer's devil; he is pictured here
at age fifteen holding a composing stick with his name in wood type. At
fifty he founded his own publishing house, Charles L. Webster & Company, which brought out many of his late works, including *Huckleberry
Finn*. From the start the firm was mismanaged, and Clemens poured
most of its profits into an entrepreneurial folly, the Paige Typsetter, an
imperfect forerunner of the Linotype. In 1895 he went bust, and most of
his following years were one long struggle back to solvency.

Daguerreotype courtesy of the Mark Twain Project, Bancroft Library

TITLE _____

AUTHOR _____

DATE READ _____

COMMENTS _____

_____

_____

_____

_____

_____

_____

_____

_____

_____

_____

_____

_____

_____

_____

_____

_____

_____

_____

_____

_____

_____

_____

_____

_____

_____

_____

_____

_____

_____

TITLE _____

AUTHOR _____

DATE READ _____

COMMENTS _____

_____

_____

_____

_____

_____

_____

_____

_____

_____

_____

_____

_____

_____

_____

_____

_____

_____

_____

_____

_____

_____

_____

_____

_____

_____

_____

_____

_____

TITLE _____

AUTHOR _____

DATE READ _____

COMMENTS _____

_____

_____

_____

_____

_____

_____

_____

_____

_____

_____

_____

_____

_____

_____

_____

_____

_____

_____

_____

_____

_____

_____

_____

_____

_____

As an Amherst undergraduate, Henry Clay Folger (1857–1930), later chairman of the board of Standard Oil Company, discovered the poems and plays of William Shakespeare. He took a special interest in the earliest editions of the works and made a second career of ferreting them out and trying to establish their printing history. He amassed the world's largest collection of materials by and about Shakespeare—he collected seventy copies of the First Folio of 1623 alone—and in 1928 built a research library to house it, the Folger Shakespeare Library on Washington's Capitol Hill. The library's Reading Room is shown here.

Photograph courtesy of the Folger Shakespeare Library

TITLE _____

AUTHOR _____

DATE READ _____

COMMENTS _____

_____

_____

_____

_____

_____

_____

_____

_____

_____

Sixteenth Century Bookmaking

The Engraver

The Typecaster

TITLE _____

AUTHOR _____

DATE READ _____

COMMENTS _____

_____

_____

_____

_____

_____

_____

_____

_____

_____

Engravings by Jost Amman (1568)

The Printer   The Bookbinder

TITLE _____

AUTHOR _____

DATE READ _____

COMMENTS _____

_____

_____

_____

_____

_____

_____

_____

_____

_____

_____

_____

_____

_____

_____

_____

_____

_____

_____

_____

_____

_____

_____

_____

_____

_____

_____

_____

TITLE _____

AUTHOR _____

DATE READ _____

COMMENTS _____

_____

_____

_____

_____

_____

_____

_____

_____

_____

_____

_____

_____

_____

_____

_____

_____

_____

_____

_____

_____

_____

_____

_____

_____

TITLE _____

AUTHOR _____

DATE READ _____

COMMENTS _____

_____

_____

_____

_____

_____

_____

_____

_____

_____

_____

_____

_____

_____

_____

_____

_____

_____

_____

_____

_____

_____

_____

_____

_____

_____

California railroad tycoon Henry E. Huntington (1850–1927) retired from business in 1908 to live out his dream: to build a personal book collection rivaling the greatest European national libraries. In less than twenty years he acquired tens of thousands of the earliest English and American books and established the Huntington Library of San Marino as a world center for the study of printing history. His purchases included a Gutenberg Bible, twenty-five Caxtons, and the manuscript of Ben Franklin's autobiography.

Photograph by Arnold Genthe, courtesy of the Huntington Library

TITLE _____

AUTHOR _____

DATE READ _____

COMMENTS _____

_____

_____

_____

_____

_____

_____

_____

_____

_____

_____

_____

_____

_____

_____

_____

_____

_____

The first bookmobiles, horse-drawn carriages lined with shelves of odd volumes, appeared in England in the late nineteenth century to provide books to families remote from any circulating collection. America adopted the idea, and by the early twenties "traveling branches" had become a permanent feature of many larger city libraries. Pictured is one of the earliest motorized models, the bookmobile that began serving readers on the fringes of Evanston, Illinois, on June 21, 1920.

Photograph courtesy of the Evanston Public Library

TITLE _____

AUTHOR _____

DATE READ _____

COMMENTS _____

_____

_____

_____

_____

_____

_____

_____

_____

_____

_____

_____

_____

_____

EVANSTON PUBLIC LIBRARY
USE OF BOOKS FREE

TITLE _____

AUTHOR _____

DATE READ _____

COMMENTS _____

_____

_____

_____

_____

_____

_____

_____

_____

_____

_____

_____

_____

_____

_____

_____

_____

_____

_____

_____

_____

_____

_____

_____

_____

_____

_____

_____

TITLE _____

AUTHOR _____

DATE READ _____

COMMENTS _____

_____

_____

_____

_____

_____

_____

_____

_____

_____

_____

_____

_____

_____

_____

_____

_____

_____

_____

_____

_____

_____

_____

_____

_____

_____

TITLE _____

AUTHOR _____

DATE READ _____

COMMENTS _____

_____

_____

_____

_____

_____

_____

_____

_____

_____

_____

_____

_____

_____

_____

_____

_____

_____

_____

_____

_____

_____

_____

_____

_____

Photograph by Edward Leigh, courtesy of the Provost and Scholars of King's College, Cambridge

"You are soon in my library and soon out of it, for most of the books are contained in a single room. . . . Round the walls are a dozen wooden bookcases of various heights and shapes, a couple of them well designed, the others cheap. In the middle of the room stands a curious object: a bookcase which once belonged to my grandfather. It has in its front a little projecting shelf supported on two turned pillars of wood, and it has a highly polished back. Some say it is a converted bedstead. It stood in a similar position in the middle of his study over a hundred years ago—he was a country clergyman. Bedstead or not, it is agreeable and original, and I have tried to fill it with volumes of gravity, appropriate to its past. Here are the theological works of Isaac Barrow, thirteen volumes, full morocco, stamped with college arms. Here are the works of John Milton, five volumes, similarly garbed. Here is Evelyn's Diary in full calf, and Arnold's Thucydides, and Tacitus and Homer. Here are my grandfather's own works, bearing such titles as *One Primeval Language, The Apocalypse Its Own Interpreter* and *Mohammedanism Unveiled.* Have you read my grandfather's works? No? Have I read them? No."

E. M. Forster, from his essay "In My Library"

TITLE _____

AUTHOR _____

DATE READ _____

COMMENTS _____

_____

_____

_____

_____

_____

_____

_____

_____

_____

_____

TITLE _____

AUTHOR _____

DATE READ _____

COMMENTS _____

_____

_____

_____

_____

_____

_____

_____

_____

_____

_____

_____

_____

_____

_____

_____

_____

_____

_____

_____

_____

_____

_____

_____

_____

_____

_____

_____

_____

_____

Drawing by O. Soglow, © 1967 The New Yorker Magazine, Inc.

TITLE _____

AUTHOR _____

DATE READ _____

COMMENTS _____

_____

_____

_____

_____

_____

_____

_____

_____

_____

_____

_____

_____

_____

_____

_____

_____

_____

_____

_____

_____

_____

_____

_____

_____

_____

_____

TITLE _____

AUTHOR _____

DATE READ _____

COMMENTS _____

_____

_____

_____

_____

_____

_____

_____

_____

_____

_____

_____

_____

_____

_____

_____

_____

_____

_____

_____

_____

_____

_____

_____

_____

_____

_____

_____

_____

In 1879, the Scottish philologist James Murray signed a contract with Oxford University Press to plan and edit a new English dictionary. The book, the contract stipulated, was to not exceed seven thousand pages and was to be produced within ten years; it grew to over sixteen thousand pages and was not completed until 1933, fifty-four years after work on it began. Murray's *Oxford English Dictionary*, expanding still, is a glory of the language, the most inclusive and historically accurate of all dictionaries, the supreme authority on the use of English words from 1066 to the present.

Photograph courtesy of K. M. Elisabeth Murray, © 1977 by Yale University Press

TITLE _____

AUTHOR _____

DATE READ _____

COMMENTS _____

_____

_____

_____

_____

_____

_____

_____

_____

_____

_____

_____

_____

_____

_____

_____

_____

_____

_____

_____

_____

_____

_____

_____

_____

_____

_____

TITLE _____

AUTHOR _____

DATE READ _____

COMMENTS _____

_____

_____

_____

_____

_____

_____

_____

_____

_____

_____

_____

_____

_____

With the arrival of the printing press, which for the first time made books of all kinds generally available, the Roman Catholic Church found it necessary to compile a list of books dangerous to the morals and faith of its members. In 1559, the Sacred Congregation of the Roman Inquisition published the *Index Librorum Prohibitorum*—the *Index of Forbidden Books*—a catalogue of works not to be read by Catholics. The *Index*, revised and supplemented frequently, listed not only books prohibited by canon law—books heretical, obscene, or dealing with magic— but also books considered by the Inquisition to be basically sound but in places to stray from the tenets of the Church. Such books could be read but only if "corrected"—that is, if first censored by a Church official in the manner prescribed for the book in the *Index*. Pictured is a copy of a Spanish translation of Voltaire's *Histoire de Charles XII* printed in Madrid in 1740. On the verso of the title page of the second volume is a certificate dated September 17, 1798, declaring the copy "corrected and expurgated as required by the Index of 1790"; the book's prohibited passages were brushed over with ink. The *Index* went through twenty editions, the last in 1948, before the Vatican announced suspension of its publication in 1966.

Photographs courtesy of the Houghton Library, Harvard University

TITLE _____

AUTHOR _____

DATE READ _____

COMMENTS _____

_____

_____

_____

_____

_____

_____

_____

_____

_____

_____

_____

_____

_____

_____

_____

_____

_____

_____

_____

_____

_____

_____

_____

_____

_____

_____

_____

TITLE _____

AUTHOR _____

DATE READ _____

COMMENTS _____

_____

_____

_____

_____

_____

_____

_____

_____

_____

_____

_____

_____

_____

_____

_____

_____

_____

_____

_____

_____

_____

_____

_____

_____

_____

_____

TITLE _____

AUTHOR _____

DATE READ _____

COMMENTS _____

_____

_____

_____

_____

_____

_____

_____

_____

_____

_____

_____

_____

_____

_____

_____

_____

_____

_____

_____

_____

_____

_____

_____

_____

_____

Drawing by Saxon, © 1977 The New Yorker Magazine, Inc.

"No, we can't play paddle tennis. We can't play anything. Richard is going to finish 'The Decline and Fall of the Roman Empire' if it kills him."

Alfred A. Knopf, founder of Borzoi Books, built a list of authors that was the envy of his competitors and a joy to readers of serious writing. He published Willa Cather, Wallace Stevens, and John Updike, and presented Thomas Mann and André Gide to America. Between 1915 and his death in 1984, he oversaw the publication of some five thousand titles, notable not only for their literary quality but for their physical attractiveness. Knopf's stringent standards for writing and book design and his fairness with authors led H. L. Mencken to call him "the perfect publisher"; John Hersey characterized him as "the sworn enemy of hogwash, bunk, gas and rubbish, and a scourge of hypocrites and shoddyites."

Photograph © 1972 by Tom Hollyman, courtesy of Alfred A. Knopf, Inc.

TITLE _____

AUTHOR _____

DATE READ _____

COMMENTS _____

_____

_____

_____

_____

_____

_____

_____

_____

_____

_____

_____

_____

_____

_____

_____

_____

_____

_____

_____

_____

_____

_____

_____

_____

_____

_____

_____

_____

_____

TITLE _____

AUTHOR _____

DATE READ _____

COMMENTS _____

_____

_____

_____

_____

_____

_____

_____

_____

_____

_____

_____

_____

_____

_____

_____

_____

_____

_____

_____

_____

_____

_____

_____

_____

_____

_____

TITLE _____

AUTHOR _____

DATE READ _____

COMMENTS _____

_____

_____

_____

_____

_____

_____

_____

_____

_____

_____

_____

_____

_____

_____

_____

_____

_____

_____

_____

_____

_____

_____

_____

_____

_____

_____

TITLE _____

AUTHOR _____

DATE READ _____

COMMENTS _____

_____

_____

_____

_____

_____

_____

_____

_____

_____

_____

_____

_____

_____

_____

_____

_____

_____

_____

_____

_____

_____

_____

_____

_____

_____

_____

_____

_____

TITLE _____

AUTHOR _____

DATE READ _____

COMMENTS _____

_____

_____

_____

_____

_____

_____

_____

_____

In 1925, Donald Klopfer, fresh from Columbia College, and his classmate, Bennett Cerf, bought the Modern Library from Cerf's boss, publisher Horace Liveright. By 1927, wrote Cerf, "we were talking about doing a few books on the side, when suddenly I got an inspiration and said, 'I've got the name for our publishing house. We just said we were going to publish a few books on the side at random. Let's call it Random House.'

"Donald liked it, and Rockwell Kent [the popular graphic artist] said, 'That's a great name. I'll draw your trademark.' So, sitting at my desk, he took a piece of paper and in five minutes drew Random House, which has been our colophon ever since."

Bennett Cerf, from his memoir, At Random

"Just think! Every book that's ever been published in the United States is right here in the Library of Congress." "Even 'The Poky Little Puppy'?"

TITLE _____

AUTHOR _____

DATE READ _____

COMMENTS _____

_____

_____

_____

_____

_____

_____

_____

_____

_____

_____

_____

_____

_____

_____

_____

_____

_____

_____

The Library of Congress, America's national library, was created by order of President John Adams in 1800. The first items in the collection came from England in eleven hair trunks and a map case and were housed in a room in the Capitol. The collection now occupies three buildings on Capitol Hill, contains eighty million items, and grows by one and a half million items per year, ten items each working minute. It includes four million maps, ten million prints and photographs, and twenty million books and pamphlets—not to mention a first edition of Janette Sebring Lowrey's *Poky Little Puppy*.

Drawing by Charles E. Martin, © 1971 The New Yorker Magazine, Inc.

TITLE _____

AUTHOR _____

DATE READ _____

COMMENTS _____

_____

_____

_____

_____

_____

_____

_____

_____

_____

_____

_____

_____

_____

_____

_____

_____

_____

_____

_____

_____

_____

_____

_____

_____

_____

_____

_____

TITLE

AUTHOR

DATE READ

COMMENTS

TITLE _____

AUTHOR _____

DATE READ _____

COMMENTS _____

_____

_____

_____

_____

_____

_____

_____

_____

_____

_____

_____

_____

_____

_____

_____

_____

_____

_____

_____

_____

_____

_____

_____

_____

_____

_____

_____

Perhaps no other book editor did more to shape American literature—or his profession—than Maxwell Perkins (1884–1947). An editor at Charles Scribner's Sons, he guided into print many of the greatest writers of his lifetime, among them F. Scott Fitzgerald, Ernest Hemingway, Ring Lardner, and Thomas Wolfe. His ability to intuit greatness and elicit it from his authors—to, in his own words, "release energy"—is legend, and his example a tremendous influence on those of his successors who believe, as he did, that "there could be nothing so important as a book can be."

Photograph courtesy of Charles Scribner's Sons, Inc.

Steel king and philanthropist Andrew Carnegie (1835–1919) was born the son of a poor but scholarly weaver in Dumferline, Scotland. Like his father, who with his personal library helped found his town's library, Carnegie was largely self-educated and believed passionately in the need for communities to make available to their residents the knowledge to be had through books. In his later years, having made hundreds of millions of dollars in U.S. industry, he personally provided for the erection of 2,507 free public libraries, most of them in America and many of them named in his honor.

Caricature by Peter Newell, courtesy of the Houghton Library, Harvard University

TITLE _____

AUTHOR _____

DATE READ _____

COMMENTS _____

_____

_____

_____

_____

_____

_____

_____

_____

_____

_____

_____

_____

_____

_____

_____

_____

_____

_____

_____

_____

_____

_____

_____

_____

_____

_____

_____

TITLE _____

AUTHOR _____

DATE READ _____

COMMENTS _____

_____

_____

_____

_____

_____

_____

_____

_____

_____

_____

_____

_____

_____

_____

_____

_____

_____

_____

_____

_____

_____

_____

_____

_____

_____

TITLE _____

AUTHOR _____

DATE READ _____

COMMENTS _____

_____

_____

_____

_____

_____

_____

_____

_____

_____

_____

_____

_____

_____

_____

_____

_____

_____

_____

_____

_____

_____

_____

_____

_____

_____

_____

_____

Sea-eagle said to him: "Here am I well honoured and measurelessly happy; and I have a message for thee from the King". "What is it?" said Hallblithe; but he deemed that he knew what it would be, and he reddened for the joy of his assured hope. Said the Sea-eagle: "Joy to thee, O shipmate! I am to take thee to the place where thy beloved abideth, & there shalt thou see her, but not so as she can see thee; & thereafter shalt thou go to the King, that thou mayst tell him if she shall accomplish thy desire". Then was Hallblithe glad beyond measure, & his heart danced within him, & he deemed it but meet that the others should be so joyous and blithe with him, for they led him along without any delay, and were glad at his rejoicing; and words failed him to tell of his gladness.

But as he went, the thoughts of his coming converse with his beloved curled sweetly round his heart, so that scarce anything had seemed so sweet to him before; & he fell a-pondering what they twain, he and the Hostage, should do when they came together again; whether they should abide on the Glittering Plain, or go back again to Cleveland by the Sea and dwell in the House of the Kindred; and for his part he yearned to behold the roof of his fathers and to tread the meadow which his scythe had swept, and the acres where his hook had smitten the wheat. But he said to himself: "I will wait till I hear her desire hereon". Now they went into the wood at the back of the King's pavilion and through it, and so over the hill, and beyond it came into a land of hills and dales exceeding fair and lovely; and a river wound about the dales, lap-

Chapter XIII. Hallblithe beholdeth the woman who loveth him.

But on the morrow the men arose, & the Sea-eagle and his damsel came to Hallblithe; for the other two damsels were departed, and the

g 3   85

William Morris, the poet, craftsman, and social critic, loathed the industrialization of the Victorian age and turned to medieval England for models for his art and way of life. He deeply believed that man's happiness lies in doing meaningful work with the hands, and he found his own greatest happiness and perhaps his most meaningful work in planning the fifty-two hand-printed publications of London's Kelmscott Press. Founded in 1891 and closed in 1898, two years after Morris's death, Kelmscott had a short life but initiated the great tradition of fine private press printing that continues to this day. Above is a spread from Morris's own romance *The Story of the Glittering Plain*, the printing of which, in an edition of 257 copies, was completed in February 1894. Morris designed the type, borders, and initials; the engraving is one of twenty-three made for the book by Walter Crane. *Courtesy of the Library of Congress*

TITLE _____

AUTHOR _____

DATE READ _____

COMMENTS _____

_____

_____

_____

_____

_____

_____

_____

_____

_____

_____

_____

_____

_____

_____

_____

_____

_____

_____

_____

_____

_____

_____

_____

_____

_____

_____

_____

_____

TITLE _____

AUTHOR _____

DATE READ _____

COMMENTS _____

_____

_____

_____

_____

_____

_____

_____

_____

_____

_____

_____

_____

_____

_____

_____

_____

_____

_____

_____

_____

_____

_____

_____

_____

_____

TITLE _____

AUTHOR _____

DATE READ _____

COMMENTS _____

_____

_____

_____

_____

_____

_____

_____

_____

_____

_____

_____

_____

_____

_____

_____

_____

_____

_____

_____

_____

_____

_____

_____

_____

_____

_____

_____

_____

TITLE _____

AUTHOR _____

DATE READ _____

COMMENTS _____

_____

_____

_____

_____

_____

_____

_____

_____

_____

_____

_____

_____

The seven hundred books of Bruce Rogers (1870–1957) go unchallenged as the most various and significant body of work by an American typographer. Each Rogers book is a unique entity, an idiosyncratic answer to the typographic problems posed by its text, but there is nothing strained about each book's difference from the others, nothing preciously "novel." Rogers's genius lay in his bottomless resourcefulness, an intuitive gift for the arrangement of letter and ornament matched by a remarkable knowl-

TITLE _____

AUTHOR _____

DATE READ _____

COMMENTS _____

_____

_____

_____

_____

_____

_____

_____

_____

_____

_____

_____

_____

edge of the five centuries of printing before him. There was never a typographer more alive to the design possibilities of the book.

Rogers was a college student in Indiana when the Kelmscott books were new, and it was Morris's work that sparked his interest in the book arts. In 1896, he moved to Boston and began a long relationship with the Riverside Press; he was later associated with a number of private presses in both America and England, and with the university presses of Harvard and Cambridge. His masterpiece, the Oxford Lectern Bible, a folio edition of the King James Version set in Centaur, one of the two fonts designed by Rogers, was four years in production and completed in 1935. The printing scholar Joseph Blumenthal considers it the most important printed book of the twentieth century.

TITLE _____

AUTHOR _____

DATE READ _____

COMMENTS _____

_____

_____

_____

_____

_____

_____

_____

_____

_____

_____

_____

_____

_____

_____

_____

_____

_____

_____

In January 1924, Dick Simon (right) and Max Schuster started a publishing business with six thousand dollars and not one idea for a book. Simon's Aunt Wixie, an addict of newspaper puzzle pages, suggested they start with a collection of crosswords, a new kind of brainteaser then just catching on in the Sunday New York *World*. The young men, against the advice of friends in the business, took a risk on a few thousand copies of *The Crossword Puzzle Book*. It rocketed to the top of the best-seller list and by December it and its three hastily packaged sequels had made Simon & Schuster a legend—a first-year company with only four titles but over a million books in print.

Used with permission of Macmillan Publishing Company from Turning the Pages *by Peter Schwed. Copyright © 1984 by Peter Schwed*

TITLE _____

AUTHOR _____

DATE READ _____

COMMENTS _____

_____

_____

_____

_____

_____

_____

_____

_____

_____

TITLE _____

AUTHOR _____

DATE READ _____

COMMENTS _____

_____

_____

_____

_____

_____

_____

_____

_____

_____

_____

_____

_____

_____

_____

_____

_____

_____

_____

_____

"My love for the alphabet, which endures, grew out of reciting it but, before that, out of seeing the letters on the page. In my own story books, before I could read them for myself, I fell in love with various winding, enchanted-looking initials drawn by Walter Crane at the heads of fairy tales. In 'Once upon a time,' an 'O' had a rabbit running it as a treadmill, his feet upon flowers. When the day came, years later, for me to see the Book of Kells, all the wizardry of letter, initial, and word swept over me a thousand times over, and the illumination, the gold, seemed a part of the word's beauty and holiness that had been there from the start."

Eudora Welty, from her memoir, One Writer's Beginnings

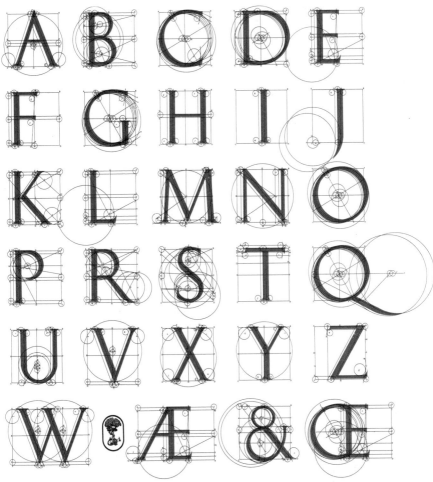

QUO·USQUE·TANDEM·ABUTERE·CATALINA·PATIENTIA·NOSTRA·
QUAM·DIU·ETIAM·FUROR·ISTE·TUUS·NOS·ELUDET·QUEM·AD·FINE
M·SESE·EFFRENATA·JACTABIT·AUDACIA·NIHILNE·TE·NOCTURNUM·
PRÆSIDIUM·PALATI·NIHIL·URBIS·VIGILIÆ·NIHIL·TIMOR·POPULI·NIHIL·
CONCURSUS·BONORUM·OMNIUM·NIHIL·HIC·MUNITISSIMUS·HABEN
DI·SENATUS·LOCUS·NIHIL·HORUM·ORA·VULTUSQUE·MOVERUNT·PA
TERE·TUA·CONSILIA·NON·SENTIS·CONSTRICTAM·JAM·OMNIUM · H
ORUM·SCIENTIA·TENERI·CONJURATIONEM·TUAM·NONKWXYZ&Œ

A Constructed Roman Alphabet *by David Lance Goines (1979), courtesy of the artist*

TITLE _____

AUTHOR _____

DATE READ _____

COMMENTS _____

_____

_____

_____

_____

_____

_____

_____

_____

_____

_____

_____

_____

_____

_____

_____

_____

_____

_____

_____

_____

_____

_____

_____

_____

_____

TITLE _____

AUTHOR _____

DATE READ _____

COMMENTS _____

_____

_____

_____

_____

_____

_____

_____

_____

_____

_____

_____

_____

_____

_____

_____

_____

_____

_____

_____

_____

_____

_____

_____

_____

_____

_____

_____

_____

TITLE _____

AUTHOR _____

DATE READ _____

COMMENTS _____

_____

_____

_____

_____

_____

_____

_____

_____

_____

_____

_____

_____

_____

_____

_____

_____

_____

_____

_____

Sylvia Beach, an American in Paris, opened her Left Bank bookshop, Shakespeare & Company, on November 19, 1919. It became a haven for the expatriated writers of the twenties, including Ezra Pound, Ernest Hemingway, Gertrude Stein, Sherwood Anderson, F. Scott Fitzgerald, and, of course, James Joyce—whose masterpiece *Ulysses* she believed in so ardently that she published it herself.

Photograph courtesy of Princeton University Library

TITLE _____

AUTHOR _____

DATE READ _____

COMMENTS _____

_____

_____

_____

_____

_____

_____

_____

_____

_____

_____

_____

_____

_____

_____

_____

_____

_____

_____

_____

_____

_____

_____

_____

_____

_____

_____

_____

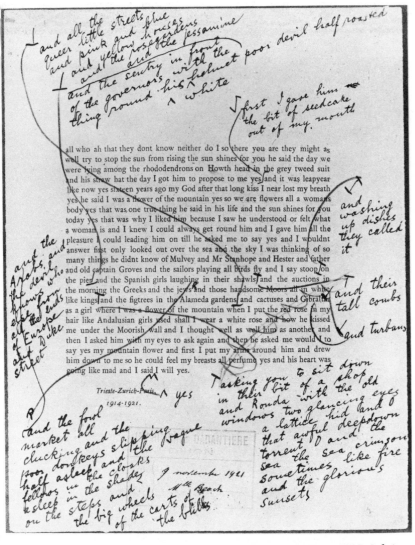

James Joyce wrote and rewrote *Ulysses* from 1914 to 1921. In 1920, Sylvia Beach had set in type what she thought was a final draft but, in the words of Joyce biographer Richard Ellmann, "with Joyce the reading of proof was a creative act. . . . [He] made innumerable changes, almost always additions, in the text [and] the book grew by one third in proof." Pictured is proof of the last page of the novel with Joyce's manuscript corrections; Joyce's crabbed handwriting and the repeated breaking up and resetting of type ended in over five thousand printer's errors in the first edition.

Courtesy of the Houghton Library, Harvard University

TITLE _____

AUTHOR _____

DATE READ _____

COMMENTS _____

_____

_____

_____

_____

_____

_____

_____

_____

_____

_____

_____

_____

_____

_____

_____

_____

_____

_____

_____

_____

_____

_____

_____

_____

_____

_____

_____

TITLE _____

AUTHOR _____

DATE READ _____

COMMENTS _____

_____

_____

_____

_____

_____

_____

_____

_____

_____

_____

_____

_____

_____

_____

_____

_____

_____

_____

_____

_____

_____

_____

_____

_____

_____

_____

For the purpose of this discussion, it is desirable to separate the purely *logical* concept of being *from the actual* fact of existence—*without, of course, forgetting that the two are related through the* will to be, *which manifests itself in the subrational* act of willing. *Thus we avoid the pitfall presented by the confusion of* I will *with* I am, *though, to be sure, another danger lurks in the negation of* I am *through the purely pragmatic concept of the* will-to-be *as part of the* will-be. *Note, however (Appendix IX, pp. 439–467), that Grüssboscher proceeds on the assumption, erroneous in our opinion, that* . . .

TITLE _____

AUTHOR _____

DATE READ _____

COMMENTS _____

_____

_____

_____

_____

_____

_____

_____

_____

_____

_____

_____

_____

_____

_____

_____

_____

_____

_____

_____

_____

_____

_____

_____

_____

_____

_____

_____

Drawing by Gluyas Williams, © 1942, 1970, The New Yorker Magazine, Inc.

TITLE _____

AUTHOR _____

DATE READ _____

COMMENTS _____

_____

_____

_____

_____

_____

_____

_____

_____

_____

_____

_____

_____

_____

_____

_____

_____

_____

_____

_____

_____

_____

_____

_____

_____

_____

_____

_____

GOUDY FLEURONS

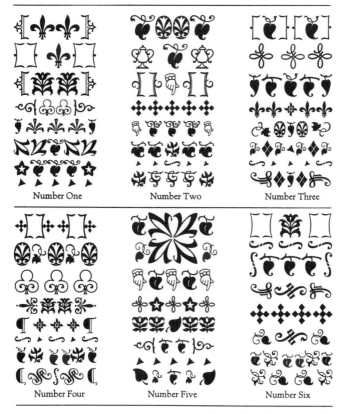

Number One

Number Two

Number Three

Number Four

Number Five

Number Six

Designed by Frederic W. Goudy, these handy fonts of dingbats are just the thing for spots and occasional decoration. Only $1.00 per font CASH.

CONTINENTAL TYPEFOUNDERS ASSOCIATION, INC.
228 East Forty-fifth Street, New York City

Frederic W. Goudy, born in Illinois in 1865, designed some one hundred fonts in his eighty-two years, an output surpassed only by Bodoni. His excellent popular writings on typography, his great commercial success, and a winning public personality combined to make him a national celebrity: more than any other person, he raised public awareness of the craftsmen behind each printed book. He also excelled as a designer of fleurons, the little "flowers" typographers use to ornament their work.

Drawing courtesy of the Library of Congress

TITLE _____

AUTHOR _____

DATE READ _____

COMMENTS _____

_____

_____

_____

_____

_____

_____

_____

_____

_____

_____

_____

_____

_____

_____

_____

_____

_____

_____

_____

_____

_____

_____

_____

_____

_____

_____

_____

_____

_____

TITLE _____

AUTHOR _____

DATE READ _____

COMMENTS _____

_____

_____

_____

_____

_____

_____

_____

_____

_____

_____

_____

_____

_____

_____

_____

_____

_____

_____

_____

_____

_____

_____

_____

_____

_____

_____

_____

_____

TITLE _____

AUTHOR _____

DATE READ _____

COMMENTS _____

_____

_____

_____

_____

_____

_____

_____

_____

_____

_____

_____

_____

_____

_____

_____

_____

_____

_____

_____

_____

_____

_____

_____

_____

_____

_____

Photograph by Phyllis Cerf Wagner, courtesy of Harold Ober Associates

"My grandfather had a moderate though reasonably diffuse and catholic library; I realize now that I got most of my early education in it. It was a little limited in its fiction content, since his taste was for simple straightforward romantic excitement like Scott or Dumas. But there was a heterogeneous scattering of other volumes, chosen apparently at random and by my grandmother, since the flyleaves bore her name and the dates in the 1880's and '90's of that time when even in a town as big as Memphis, Tennessee, ladies stopped in their carriages in the street in front of the stores and shops, and clerks and even proprietors came out to receive their commands—that time when women did most of the book-buying and the reading too, naming their children Byron and Clarissa and St. Elmo and Lothair after the romantic and tragic heroes and heroines and the even more romantic creators of them."

William Faulkner, from his foreword to The Faulkner Reader

TITLE _____

AUTHOR _____

DATE READ _____

COMMENTS _____

_____

_____

_____

_____

_____

_____

_____

_____

TITLE _____

AUTHOR _____

DATE READ _____

COMMENTS _____

_____

_____

_____

_____

_____

_____

_____

_____

_____

_____

_____

_____

_____

Every book lover has a favorite bookshop, and one may be lucky enough to have a friend or two among that shop's staff, but it is doubtful many are as fortunate as was Helene Hanff, a New York writer who for twenty years enjoyed a fully requited if long-distance romance with Marks & Company, one of London's many great secondhand booksellers. Miss Hanff set tough challenges for her book hunters, and sometimes teased them for their "slothfulness" in fulfilling her orders, but more often she praised them for finding her exquisite and inexpensive editions, and rewarded them with gifts of food at Easter and Christmas. She didn't make it to London until 1971, and by then the bookshop had closed, but she knew Marks & Company intimately from the letters of its staff of the 1950s and 1960s, a delightful correspondence collected in the volume named for the shop's address, *84, Charing Cross Road*.

Photograph by Alec Bolton, courtesy of Leo Marks

TITLE _____

AUTHOR _____

DATE READ _____

COMMENTS _____

_____

_____

_____

_____

_____

_____

_____

_____

_____

_____

_____

_____

_____

_____

_____

_____

_____

_____

_____

_____

_____

_____

_____

_____

_____

_____

TITLE _____

AUTHOR _____

DATE READ _____

COMMENTS _____

_____

_____

_____

_____

_____

_____

_____

_____

_____

_____

_____

_____

_____

_____

_____

_____

_____

_____

_____

_____

_____

_____

_____

_____

_____

_____

The Dun Emer Press of Dundrum, County Dublin, was one of Ireland's most important private presses. Founded in 1902 by Elizabeth and Lily Yeats, sisters of the poet William Butler Yeats, the press, managed and staffed entirely by women, was in operation for over fifty years. It printed a number of significant works of modern Irish literature, including books by Lady Gregory, Oliver Saint John Gogarty, and J. M. Synge. This photograph, from its earliest period, pictures Elizabeth Yeats operating an Albion hand press. *Photograph courtesy of the Saint Bride Printing Library*

TITLE _____

AUTHOR _____

DATE READ _____

COMMENTS _____

_____

_____

_____

_____

_____

_____

_____

_____

_____

_____

_____

_____

_____

_____

_____

_____

_____

_____

_____

_____

_____

_____

_____

_____

_____

_____

_____

TITLE _____

AUTHOR _____

DATE READ _____

COMMENTS _____

_____

_____

_____

_____

_____

_____

_____

_____

_____

_____

_____

_____

_____

_____

_____

_____

_____

_____

_____

_____

_____

_____

_____

_____

_____

Michael McCurdy (1942–) is prominent among contemporary craftsmen devoted to bookmaking. As founder of Penmæn Press and publisher and designer of both limited and commercial editions he has contributed significantly to recent American printing; as a wood engraver, he is perhaps the most important artist of his generation to work with the tools of such great book illustrators as Lynd Ward, Leonard Baskin, and Rockwell Kent.

Wood-engraved self-portrait of Michael McCurdy, courtesy of the artist

TITLE _____

AUTHOR _____

DATE READ _____

COMMENTS _____

_____

_____

_____

_____

_____

_____

_____

_____

_____

_____

_____

_____

_____

_____

_____

_____

_____

_____

_____

_____

_____

_____

_____

_____

_____

_____

_____

_____

TITLE _____

AUTHOR _____

DATE READ _____

COMMENTS _____

_____

_____

_____

_____

_____

_____

_____

_____

_____

_____

_____

_____

_____

_____

_____

_____

_____

_____

_____

_____

_____

_____

_____

_____

_____

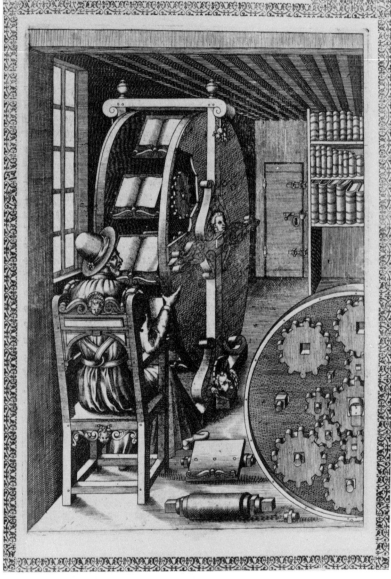

FIGVRE CLXXXVIII.

Engraving from Agostino Ramelli's Le diverse et artificiose machine del capitano Agostino
Ramelli *(Paris, 1588), courtesy of the Houghton Library, Harvard University*

Books to Read

TITLE _____

AUTHOR _____

RECOMMENDED BY _____

COMMENTS _____

_____

_____

_____

_____

_____

TITLE _____

AUTHOR _____

RECOMMENDED BY _____

COMMENTS _____

_____

_____

_____

_____

_____

TITLE _____

AUTHOR _____

RECOMMENDED BY _____

COMMENTS _____

_____

_____

_____

_____

_____

Books to Read

TITLE _____

AUTHOR _____

RECOMMENDED BY _____

COMMENTS _____

_____

_____

_____

_____

_____

TITLE _____

AUTHOR _____

RECOMMENDED BY _____

COMMENTS _____

_____

_____

_____

_____

_____

TITLE _____

AUTHOR _____

RECOMMENDED BY _____

COMMENTS _____

_____

_____

_____

_____

_____

Books to Read

TITLE _____

AUTHOR _____

RECOMMENDED BY _____

COMMENTS _____

_____

_____

_____

_____

_____

TITLE _____

AUTHOR _____

RECOMMENDED BY _____

COMMENTS _____

_____

_____

_____

_____

_____

TITLE _____

AUTHOR _____

RECOMMENDED BY _____

COMMENTS _____

_____

_____

_____

_____

_____

Books to Read

TITLE _____

AUTHOR _____

RECOMMENDED BY _____

COMMENTS _____

_____

_____

_____

_____

_____

TITLE _____

AUTHOR _____

RECOMMENDED BY _____

COMMENTS _____

_____

_____

_____

_____

_____

TITLE _____

AUTHOR _____

RECOMMENDED BY _____

COMMENTS _____

_____

_____

_____

_____

_____

Books to Read

TITLE _____

AUTHOR _____

RECOMMENDED BY _____

COMMENTS _____

_____

_____

_____

_____

_____

TITLE _____

AUTHOR _____

RECOMMENDED BY _____

COMMENTS _____

_____

_____

_____

_____

_____

TITLE _____

AUTHOR _____

RECOMMENDED BY _____

COMMENTS _____

_____

_____

_____

_____

_____

_____

Books to Read

TITLE _____

AUTHOR _____

RECOMMENDED BY_____

COMMENTS _____

_____

_____

_____

_____

_____

TITLE _____

AUTHOR _____

RECOMMENDED BY_____

COMMENTS _____

_____

_____

_____

_____

_____

TITLE _____

AUTHOR _____

RECOMMENDED BY_____

COMMENTS _____

_____

_____

_____

_____

_____

Books to Read

TITLE _____

AUTHOR _____

RECOMMENDED BY _____

COMMENTS _____

_____

_____

_____

_____

_____

TITLE _____

AUTHOR _____

RECOMMENDED BY _____

COMMENTS _____

_____

_____

_____

_____

_____

TITLE _____

AUTHOR _____

RECOMMENDED BY _____

COMMENTS _____

_____

_____

_____

_____

_____

Books Borrowed

TITLE _____

AUTHOR _____

BORROWED FROM _____

_____

_____

_____

TITLE _____

AUTHOR _____

BORROWED FROM _____

_____

_____

TITLE _____

AUTHOR _____

BORROWED FROM _____

_____

_____

_____

TITLE _____

AUTHOR _____

BORROWED FROM _____

_____

_____

TITLE _____

AUTHOR _____

BORROWED FROM _____

_____

_____

_____

Books Borrowed

TITLE _____

AUTHOR _____

BORROWED FROM _____

_____

_____

_____

TITLE _____

AUTHOR _____

BORROWED FROM _____

_____

_____

TITLE _____

AUTHOR _____

BORROWED FROM _____

_____

_____

TITLE _____

AUTHOR _____

BORROWED FROM _____

_____

_____

TITLE _____

AUTHOR _____

BORROWED FROM _____

_____

_____

_____

Books Loaned

TITLE _____

AUTHOR _____

LOANED TO _____

_____

_____

_____

TITLE _____

AUTHOR _____

LOANED TO _____

_____

_____

TITLE _____

AUTHOR _____

LOANED TO _____

_____

_____

_____

TITLE _____

AUTHOR _____

LOANED TO _____

_____

_____

TITLE _____

AUTHOR _____

LOANED TO _____

_____

_____

_____

Books Loaned

TITLE _____

AUTHOR _____

LOANED TO _____

_____

_____

_____

TITLE _____

AUTHOR _____

LOANED TO _____

_____

_____

TITLE _____

AUTHOR _____

LOANED TO _____

_____

_____

TITLE _____

AUTHOR _____

LOANED TO _____

_____

_____

TITLE _____

AUTHOR _____

LOANED TO _____

_____

_____

_____

An 1887 advertisement for the Paris publisher Epinal, courtesy of the Boston Athenæum

Bookstores

NAME _____

ADDRESS _____

_____

TELEPHONE _____

HOURS _____

_____

NAME _____

ADDRESS _____

_____

TELEPHONE _____

HOURS _____

_____

NAME _____

ADDRESS _____

_____

TELEPHONE _____

HOURS _____

_____

NAME _____

ADDRESS _____

_____

TELEPHONE _____

HOURS _____

_____

_____

Bookstores

NAME _____

ADDRESS _____

_____

TELEPHONE _____

HOURS _____

_____

NAME _____

ADDRESS _____

_____

TELEPHONE _____

HOURS _____

_____

NAME _____

ADDRESS _____

_____

TELEPHONE _____

HOURS _____

_____

NAME _____

ADDRESS _____

_____

TELEPHONE _____

HOURS _____

_____

_____

Bookstores

NAME

ADDRESS

TELEPHONE

HOURS

NAME

ADDRESS

TELEPHONE

HOURS

NAME

ADDRESS

TELEPHONE

HOURS

NAME

ADDRESS

TELEPHONE

HOURS

Libraries

NAME_____

ADDRESS_____

_____

TELEPHONE_____

HOURS_____

_____

_____

NAME_____

ADDRESS_____

_____

TELEPHONE_____

HOURS_____

_____

_____

NAME_____

ADDRESS_____

_____

TELEPHONE_____

HOURS_____

_____

_____

NAME_____

ADDRESS_____

_____

TELEPHONE_____

HOURS_____

_____

_____

Libraries

NAME _____

ADDRESS _____

_____

TELEPHONE _____

HOURS _____

_____

_____

NAME _____

ADDRESS _____

_____

TELEPHONE _____

HOURS _____

_____

_____

NAME _____

ADDRESS _____

_____

TELEPHONE _____

HOURS _____

_____

_____

NAME _____

ADDRESS _____

_____

TELEPHONE _____

HOURS _____

_____

_____

Notes

A BOOK LOVER'S JOURNAL was conceived by Ann Dilworth and Robert Lavelle. Mr. Lavelle and Christopher Carduff selected the artwork, and Mr. Carduff wrote the captions.

The text was set by Neil W. Kelley in a digitized version of Trump Mediæval, a typeface designed by West Germany's Georg Trump. The roman letters borrow from fifteenth-century Italian cuts, whereas the italics are more a biased roman than a true italic in design. As do many popular typefaces introduced since midcentury, Trump Mediæval combines the new and the classical with remarkable subtlety and in no way calls attention to its novel elements.

The book was designed by Hal Morgan and its production supervised by Lori Snell. The paper is 60-pound Glatfelter. R. R. Donnelley & Sons was the printer and binder.

Cover design by Hal Morgan.